THE AUDUBON SOCIETY POCKET GUIDES

A Chanticleer Press Edition

Text by
Joseph Wallace

Lowell W. Dingus, Ph.D., reviewer
American Museum of Natural History

Illustrations by
Donna Braginetz, Michael Cole, Brian Franczak,
Edward Heck, Douglas Henderson, Frank Ippolito,
Eleanor M. Kish, Vladimir Krb, Michael Rothman,
and Jan Sovak

FAMILIAR DINOSAURS

Alfred A. Knopf, New York

This is a Borzoi Book
Published by Alfred A. Knopf, Inc.

Copyright 1993 Chanticleer Press, Inc. All rights reserve
Published in the United States by Alfred A. Knopf, Inc.,
New York, and simultaneously in Canada by Random
House of Canada Limited, Toronto. Distributed by
Random House, Inc., New York.

Prepared and produced by Chanticleer Press, Inc.,
New York.
Typeset by Stewart, Tabori & Chang, Inc., New York,
and output by Pearl Pressman Liberty Communications
Group, Philadelphia, Pennsylvania.
Printed and bound by Tien Wah Press, Singapore.

Published May 1993
First Printing

Library of Congress Catalog Number: 92-12182
ISBN: 0-679-74150-X

Trademark "Audubon Society" used by publisher under
license from the National Audubon Society, Inc.

Cover illustration: *Triceratops* by Brian Franczak

Contents

Introduction
How to Use This Guide 6
Dinosaur Diversity 9
How Dinosaurs Lived 10
The Age of the Dinosaurs 12

The Dinosaurs 18

Appendices
Dinosaur Family Tree 174
Time Line 178
Dinosaur Skeletons 182
Index 189
Credits 191

How to Use This Guide

The fierce, meat-eating *Tyrannosaurus,* the *Apatosaurus* with its 20-foot-long neck, three-horned *Triceratops,* and other dinosaurs remain among the most intriguing ancient animals ever to walk the earth. Every year, paleontologists (the scientists who study dinosaurs and other ancient life) discover new facts about the lives and death of these magnificent reptiles. By learning to identify many of the dinosaurs, you can fully appreciate the extraordinary behavior, strength, and diversity of these remarkable creatures.

Coverage

This guide covers 78 of the most fascinating dinosaurs found worldwide, ranging from famous discoveries of a century ago to the newest and most important finds.

Organization

This easy-to-use pocket guide is divided into three parts: introductory essays; illustrated accounts of the dinosaurs; and appendices.

Introduction

Three introductory essays give you a general introduction to dinosaurs. "Dinosaur Diversity" describes the classification of the dinosaurs. "How Dinosaurs Lived" discusses current theories of dinosaur behavior, using specific examples from the book. "The Age of the Dinosaurs" traces the history of dinosaurs from their first appearance about 225 million years ago, through the 160 million years during which they were the most dominant animals on earth, to the mysterious extinction (with the exception of birds) and the controversial theories surrounding it.

The Dinosaurs This section contains 78 color paintings of dinosaurs, arranged alphabetically. These illustrations are artists' interpretations of many of the best-known dinosaur genera along with some of the lesser known, rarest, strangest, and most intriguing. Facing each illustration is a description of the genus's important physical characteristics, along with information about the areas of its fossil finds and its geologic period. The introductory paragraph reveals what paleontologists have discovered (or surmised) about the dinosaur's behavior, its feeding and breeding habits, and its close relatives. A skeletal drawing accompanies each account, to help you categorize the dinosaur.

Appendices Following the dinosaur accounts, a special section entitled "Dinosaur Skeletons" includes drawings and a brief description of dinosaur skeletons that delineate the different shapes and characteristics of various genera. The "Dinosaur Family Tree" provides a look at dinosaur classifications, and the "Time Line" gives you an overview of approximately which geologic age each dinosaur in this guide lived in.

Whether you've been a dinosaur enthusiast for years or you just want to learn about these creatures that amaze people of all ages, you'll find fascinating new information in this guide.

All dinosaurs belonged to one of two orders—Saurischia (lizard-hipped dinosaurs) or Ornithischia (bird-hipped dinosaurs), which are distinguished by differences in the structure of their hips—but they most likely evolved from the same distant ancestor. The skeletal illustrations on pages 182–188 show some of the differences among members of the two great dinosaur orders.

Saurischians

Saurischian dinosaurs encompassed two suborders: theropods, two-legged meat-eaters which included such enormous hunters as *Albertosaurus* and the smaller *Ornithomimus,* and sauropodomorphs, which included the sauropod *Camarasaurus* and other gigantic quadrupedal plant-eaters as well as the smaller and more diverse prosauropods.

Ornithischians

Ornithischian dinosaurs, all plant-eaters, included three suborders: ornithopods (such as the duck-billed dinosaur *Maiasaura*); thyreophorans (heavy-bodied ankylosaurs such as *Euoplocephalus,* stegosaurs such as *Stegosaurus,* and possibly one or two others); and marginocephalians (*Triceratops* and other horned dinosaurs as well as the pachycephalosaurs).

How Dinosaurs Lived

Dinosaur skeletons give us clues as to the behavior of the dinosaurs. For example, the serrated, knifelike teeth of *Tyrannosaurus* and other great carnivorous theropods clearly indicate that these dinosaurs ate meat. Similarly, the toothless beaks and strong, ridged cheek teeth of *Iguanodon* and other ornithopods indicate that those dinosaurs nipped off vegetation with their beaks and then ground the coarse, fibrous plant material with their specially adapted teeth.

In recent years, however, paleontologists have begun to put together a more complete picture of dinosaur life. This picture draws upon new analyses of skeletal features, studies of fossilized dinosaur footprints (called trackways), recent discoveries such as the colonial nesting sites of *Maiasaura* (complete with fossilized broken eggs and young individuals), and comparisons with modern animal behavior.

Today, many paleontologists believe that at least some of the dinosaurs were warm-blooded (controlling their body temperatures internally), unlike modern reptiles but like birds and mammals. Warm-bloodedness would have enabled *Deinonychus* and other sickle-clawed theropods, for example, to have hunted much as lions do, with a speed, agility, and stamina impossible in slower-moving cold-blooded creatures.

Maiasaura's colonial nests seem to indicate that this dinosaur lived in groups for at least part of the year and provided care to its young in the nest—behaviors more in keeping with modern mammals and birds than with reptiles. Trackways and other fossil finds have also led many scientists to theorize that other dinosaurs, including *Triceratops* and some sauropods, may have traveled in herds, perhaps migrating seasonally in search of food.

Many of the entries in this guide discuss theories of dinosaur behavior, including hunting techniques, courting and breeding behavior, and herd structure. It is important to remember, however, that in most cases these are just theories, not known facts. No one has ever seen a living dinosaur, with the exception of birds, so nearly every theory and artistic rendering detailed in this book remains controversial and most likely always will.

**The Age of
the Dinosaurs**

The dinosaurs evolved, flourished, and became extinct
during a time known as the Mesozoic Era (Era of Middle
Life), which spanned from about 250 to 66 million years ago

The Mesozoic is divided into three periods: the Triassic
(250–205 million years ago), the Jurassic (205–135 million
years ago), and the Cretaceous (135–66 million years ago)
All dinosaurs became extinct during the famous mass
extinction at the end of the Cretaceous Period.

Late Triassic Fossil records indicate that the earliest dinosaurs
appeared on earth about 225 million years ago, during
the Late Triassic. These primitive dinosaurs, including
Herrerasaurus, Staurikosaurus and, later, the
prosauropods, as well as such small, early hunters as
Coelurus, inhabited a warm, tropical environment that
contained a mix of flora and fauna that is both familiar and
strange to us today. Plants included early palms, but there
were no flowering plants or trees. Modern birds had not
yet evolved, but the first pterosaurs (flying reptiles—some
of which were enormous—with long, narrow wings) soared
the skies. The seas were populated by ichthyosaurs,
meat-eating reptiles, while ancient ancestors of today's
crocodiles inhabited lakes and swamps. Early mammals

that somewhat resembled modern shrews also inhabited that ancient world.

Jurassic Period
Both the number and variety of dinosaur genera grew tremendously as the Jurassic Period progressed. *Allosaurus* and other great meat-eating carnosaurs, smaller predators such as the coelurosaurs, and a variety of plant-eaters, including the plated dinosaurs, all thrived during the Jurassic Period. But perhaps the most spectacular denizens of the period were the mighty sauropods, some of which reached more than 100 feet in length. *Apatosaurus* (originally called *Brontosaurus*), *Diplodocus, Barosaurus,* and many others strode the continents during the Late Jurassic.

Cretaceous Period
The world that hosted the dinosaurs during the Cretaceous Period was undergoing many changes. Flowering plants and trees had evolved, and birds (some of which closely resembled their modern descendants) were increasingly numerous. Giant reptiles other than dinosaurs also thrived, including pterosaurs (some of which may have had wingspans of 50 feet) which shared the skies with the birds and long-necked, sharp-toothed plesiosaurs, which inhabited the seas.

Many of the most spectacular dinosaurs evolved during the Cretaceous Period, including *Deinonychus* and other sickle-clawed theropods; the hadrosaurs with their elaborate crests; the remarkable pachycephalosaurs, or bone-headed dinosaurs; and some of the best known of all dinosaurs, such as the carnosaur *Tyrannosaurus* and the horned dinosaur *Triceratops*. Then, within a brief geologic time, most dinosaurs (as well as the pterosaurs, plesiosaurs, and countless other plants and animals) became extinct. How they died out remains one of the greatest controversies of paleontology.

The Great Extinction

Scientists and the general public alike have long been fascinated by the seemingly sudden extinction of the dinosaurs (except birds) about 66 million years ago. Today, one of the most popular theories postulates that a giant comet or asteroid smashed into the earth, sending up a worldwide, long-lasting cloud of dust and smoke. Plants, deprived of sunlight, began to die, followed by plant-eating and, finally, meat-eating dinosaurs.

Another theory discounts the possibility of an asteroid impact, and instead points to the evidence of tremendous volcanic activity at the end of the Cretaceous Period, which

14

also resulted in the death of plants and culminated in the extinction of all dinosaurs.

Still other experts acknowledge the rampant volcanic activity of the time and even agree that an asteroid may have hit the earth, but believe that these events had only a minor role in the death of the dinosaurs. They point out that the number of dinosaur genera dwindled for many millions of years before the end of the Cretaceous Period, most likely due to long-term changes in climate and other factors. The catastrophic events that may have occurred at the end of the Cretaceous Period at most served as a final blow to the already doomed dinosaurs.

THE DINOSAURS

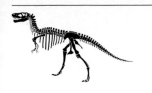

Acrocanthosaurus *Top-spined Reptile*
Saurischia; Theropoda; Carnosauria

Acrocanthosaurus belonged to a family of large carnosaurs called the spinosaurids, which were distinguished from all other meat-eating dinosaurs by the strange bony spines jutting up from their backbones. In some members of the group, such as *Spinosaurus,* the spines reached 6′ in length and probably supported great sails of skin stretching from the shoulders to the base of the tail. *Acrocanthosaurus*'s spines, however, grew to only 12″ long. Scientists think the spines may have supported a long, thin ridge of muscle down the dinosaur's back, forming a low but pronounced crest, but are not sure how this structure might have been used.

Physical Characteristics	43′ long; one of the largest carnosaurs. Thick, strong hind limbs carried its enormous weight. Toes and fingers tipped with sharp claws. Head comparatively small; jaws lined with sharp, curved teeth, flattened and serrated for the tearing of flesh.
Fossil Sites	Oklahoma, USA.
Geologic Age	Early Cretaceous.

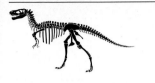

Albertosaurus *Alberta Reptile*
Saurischia; Theropoda; Carnosauria

A smaller and more lightly built relative of the
Tyrannosaurus, Albertosaurus was the most common
meat-eating dinosaur in the plains and hills of what are now
Alberta and Montana, which were also home to enormous
numbers of duckbills and other Late Cretaceous dinosaurs.
Most scientists believe that *Albertosaurus* hunted
Maiasaura and other duckbills and perhaps even battled
such well-defended dinosaurs as *Triceratops*. Albertosaurs
may have stalked the vast herds of plant-eating dinosaurs
that roamed those ancient grasslands, choosing and chasing
down weak, sick, and unwary individuals.

Physical Characteristics: 26' long. Long, muscular hind limbs; small, comparatively
weak forelimbs; two-fingered hands. In front of its eyes
may have been a pair of short triangular or rectangular
horns, and behind its eyes were a second, smaller pair.
Jaws bolstered by powerful muscles and lined with sharp,
serrated teeth.

Fossil Sites: Alberta, Canada; Montana, USA.

Geologic Age: Late Cretaceous.

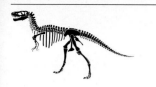

Allosaurus *Different Reptile*
Saurischia; Theropoda; Carnosauria

Almost as well known as *Tyrannosaurus,* this carnosaur lived tens of million of years earlier. It was a dominant meat-eater in what is now the Rocky Mountain region of the United States, which it shared with large populations of *Apatosaurus* and other great sauropods. Some experts believe that *Allosaurus* may have hunted in packs, because it is unlikely that this mid-size carnosaur could take on a 70′–long sauropod alone. Several allosaurs might have chosen a young or ill sauropod, then slashed at it with their razor-sharp talons and knifelike teeth until they brought it down. Several *Apatosaurus* skeletons have been found with *Allosaurus* toothmarks on their bones.

Physical Characteristics	35′ long; 1½ tons. Powerful hind limbs; small forelimbs with 3-fingered hands tipped with sharp claws; serrated teeth. Very thick but extremely flexible neck. A long bony ridge ran from between the eyes to the snout; a triangular horn sprouted just above and in front of each eye.
Fossil Sites	Rocky Mountains, USA; Tanzania, Africa; Australia.
Geologic Age	Late Jurassic/Early Cretaceous.

Anatosaurus *Duck Reptile*
Ornithischia; Ornithopoda; Hadrosauridae

When scientists unearthed the first hadrosaurids, the duck-billed dinosaurs, they assumed that these plant-eaters thrashed their laterally flattened tails to swim through swamps and lakes and ate soft aquatic vegetation with their toothless ducklike bills. Further study showed that the backs of duckbills' jaws were lined with hundreds of grinding teeth, clearly designed to tear coarse, hard plant material. Finally, scientists were able to examine the actual contents of an *Anatosaurus*'s stomach—fossilized along with the bones and skin in one of the most remarkable finds ever made—and discovered that this duckbill actually ate pine needles, as well as twigs, seeds, and other parts of plants found far from water.

Physical Characteristics	40' long; 3½ tons; one of the largest duckbills. *Anatosaurus* had no facial crest but may have had pockets of loose skin on its long-snouted, flattened face that it could inflate in display or to produce loud calls.
Fossil Sites	Alberta, Canada; Montana, New Jersey, USA.
Geologic Age	Late Cretaceous.

Anchisaurus *Near Reptile*
Saurischia; Sauropodomorpha; Prosauropoda

Prosauropods were among the earliest and most diverse dinosaurs, ranging from fleet-footed predators to lumbering plant-eaters that resembled the later sauropods. *Anchisaurus,* one of the first dinosaurs unearthed in North America, was among the smaller prosauropods, reaching no more than 7′ in length, and was one of the most lightly built of all dinosaurs. While scientists think this dinosaur inhabited dry highland areas, they are still unsure exactly what *Anchisaurus* ate. Its round, blunt teeth could have chewed either plants or flesh (or both), while the remarkably long claws on the first toes of its forefeet might have been employed to tear up plants, to shred meat, or as weapons.

Physical Characteristics	6–7′ long; shaped roughly like a small sauropod. Hind limbs longer than forelimbs; may have been comfortable walking both on hind limbs and on all fours.
Fossil Sites	Connecticut, USA; South Africa.
Geologic Age	Late Triassic/Early Jurassic.

Apatosaurus *Deceptive Reptile*
Saurischia; Sauropodomorpha; Sauropoda

Under its former name, *Brontosaurus* (Thunder Reptile), this was probably the most famous of the plant-eating dinosaurs. It has also been one of the most maligned of all the great reptiles, often described as sluggish, slow-moving, and stupid. Yet, these long-necked, long-tailed, heavy-bodied dinosaurs were apparently far more alert and active than was previously believed. Fossilized trackways indicate that sauropods may have traveled long distances in great herds or family groups, as modern elephants do. Young may have traveled in the center of the herd, obtaining greater protection from marauding predators. When attacked, adult apatosaurs may have reared onto their hind legs, using their whiplike tails and pillarlike forelimbs as lethal weapons.

Physical Characteristics	70′ long or longer; 14½′ high at the shoulder; 30 tons. Hind limbs far longer than forelimbs. Long, low skull; peglike teeth used to eat leaves and other vegetation.
Fossil Sites	Colorado, Utah, Wyoming, Oklahoma, USA.
Geologic Age	Late Jurassic.

28

Archaeopteryx *Ancient Wing*
Saurischia; Theropoda; Coelurosauria

It was with the discovery of *Archaeopteryx* that scientists first theorized that dinosaurs and modern birds were closely related. *Archaeopteryx*'s agile body, slim jaws lined with needle-sharp teeth, and other skeletal characteristics are similar to those seen in the predatory coelurosaurs and deinonychosaurs. But *Archaeopteryx* also had feathers, as well as other birdlike features that indicate it was able to fly. *Archaeopteryx* may have used its feathers for balance or for short glides as it chased insects, lizards, and other small prey, snapping them up with its toothy jaws. Most experts no longer believe that *Archaeopteryx* was the "missing link" between dinosaurs and birds; instead, it was probably an evolutionary dead end supplanted by more efficient dinosaurs and true birds.

Physical Characteristics	3′ long, including a bony feather-covered tail. Its feathered wings had 3 fingers tipped with 3 long, sharp claws; hind limbs had long, slender, clawed toes.
Fossil Sites	Bavaria, Germany.
Geologic Age	Late Jurassic.

30

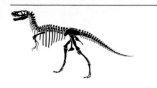

Avimimus *Bird Mimic*
Saurischia; Theropoda; Coelurosauria

Although no *Avimimus* skeletons with feathers have been found, this dinosaur's birdlike skeletal features indicate that it may have had feathers. Its 3-toed feet, muscular legs, wide hips, large eyes and brain, and toothless beak are all found in birds, but if it did have feathers, *Avimimu* would have been a very weak flyer. Most likely, it either ate plants or used its speed, agility, and intelligence to chase down insects and other small prey, while employing the same attributes to escape such equally agile and fast-moving—and far more fearsomely armed—predators as *Velociraptor*.

Physical Characteristics	5′ long; very slim and lightly built. Elongated shins and muscular thighs on hind limbs; bony, birdlike, 3-toed hind feet. Forelimbs short and clawed, possibly feathered. Toothless jaw; high-domed head.
Fossil Sites	Mongolia.
Geologic Age	Late Cretaceous.

Barosaurus *Heavy Reptile*
Saurischia; Sauropodomorpha; Sauropoda

Like *Apatosaurus* and *Diplodocus, Barosaurus* was one of the diplodocid ("double-beam") sauropods, which were extremely long but slimmer and more lightly built than such enormous sauropods as *Seismosaurus.* The largest species of *Barosaurus* was one of the longest of all sauropods. Like its relatives, *Barosaurus* probably roamed partly forested northern regions, perhaps in family groups or herds, feasting on treetop vegetation. Although very much larger than most Late Jurassic predators, *Barosaurus* may have fallen prey to large carnosaurs hunting in packs.

Physical Characteristics	90' long. Long, sloping head; snakelike neck; thick legs; skinny tail. Weak, pencil-shaped teeth set in front of jaw. Hind limbs far longer than forelimbs, probably causing its back to slope downward from the hips to the neck. Extremely long neck vertebrae (up to 3' long).
Fossil Sites	Utah, Wyoming, USA; Tanzania, Africa.
Geologic Age	Late Jurassic.

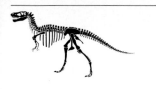

Baryonyx *Heavy Claw*
Saurischia; Theropoda; Coelurosauria or Carnosauria

This extraordinary dinosaur, first described in 1986, is placed in a family all its own. It was a meat-eater with a long, narrow skull, similar to that of a crocodile, filled with 128 teeth, twice as many as any known coelurosaur or carnosaur had. *Baryonyx* also had remarkably strong and thick forelimbs for a theropod, and each forefoot was tipped with a spectacular curved claw that grew to 12 inches in length. These physical characteristics, along with the discovery of fossilized fish in the site where *Baryonyx* was found, have led scientists to wonder what combination of tooth and claw *Baryonyx* may have used to capture its aquatic prey.

Physical Characteristics	20′ long: large for a coelurosaur, mid-size for a carnosaur. Heavy-bodied; strong hind limbs; surprisingly long forelimbs indicate that *Baryonyx* may have spent some time on all fours. Long skull had a small, bony crest; neck thick and inflexible.
Fossil Sites	England.
Geologic Age	Early Cretaceous.

Brachiosaurus *Arm Reptile*
Saurischia; Sauropodomorpha; Sauropoda

Brachiosaurus was one of the most massive of all dinosaurs. This huge sauropod, one of the heaviest animals ever to live on land, weighed at least 85 tons (almost three times as much as *Apatosaurus*), and some individuals might have reached 100 tons or more. *Brachiosaurus*'s front legs were extremely long, so its shoulders stood higher than its hips, as do those of modern-day giraffes. Scientists guess that *Brachiosaurus* used its long neck to reach succulent leaves in the tops of trees, far beyond the reach of other herbivores. The shape of its teeth suggests that it bit off and chewed leaves and other vegetation, instead of just scraping at them, as did *Diplodocus* and other sauropods with weak, peglike teeth.

Physical Characteristics	75–90′(or more) long; 85–110 tons. Very long neck, odd skull featuring bony struts that apparently served to lighten the weight; nostrils located on a bump above the eyes. Teeth strong and chisel-shaped.
Fossil Sites	Colorado, USA; Tanzania; Algeria.
Geologic Age	Late Jurassic.

38

Camarasaurus *Chambered Reptile*
Saurischia; Sauropodomorpha; Sauropoda

An unusually thickset sauropod, *Camarasaurus* got its name from the hollow "chambers" in its backbones that served to lighten its weight. Paleontologists have found skeletons of juvenile and adult camarasaurs in the same fossil beds, and some believe that this sauropod, like others, traveled in herds. *Camarasaurus* may have migrated large distances across the North American plains in search of pine needles, horsetails, and other tough vegetation, which it bit off with its thick, spoon-shaped teeth.

Physical Characteristics | 60' long; 20 tons. Tail long; neck long and flexible; body rather short and deep. Nasal openings, placed on top of the large, deep but short skull, were so huge that some experts think that this sauropod may have had a trunk like that of an elephant.

Fossil Sites | Colorado, Utah, Wyoming, Oklahoma, USA.

Geologic Age | Late Jurassic.

Camptosaurus *Bent Reptile*
Ornithischia; Ornithopoda; Camptosauridae

An early ornithopod that was similar in many ways to the familiar, later *Iguanodon, Camptosaurus* appears to have been one of the most common plant-eaters in parts of Late Jurassic North America and Europe. At first glance *Camptosaurus* looks as if it might have been a bipedal dinosaur because of its typically strong and heavy hind limbs and short, thick forelimbs. But closer study reveals that 3 toes of each forefoot were tipped in tiny hooves, suggesting that this dinosaur, like many other ornithopods, spent at least some time walking on all fours.

Physical Characteristics	Adults 20' long; juveniles as small as 4' long. Long skull; cheeks packed with ridged teeth; hard, toothless beak. Bony plate separated mouth from breathing passages, allowing *Camptosaurus* to eat and breathe at the same time.
Fossil Sites	Colorado, South Dakota, Utah, Wyoming, USA; Portugal; England.
Geologic Age	Late Jurassic.

Carnotaurus *Carnivorous Bull*
Saurischia; Theropoda; Carnosauria

When a remarkably complete and pristine *Carnotaurus* skeleton with skin impressions was unearthed in Argentina, it immediately became apparent that this was a very unusual dinosaur. Above its remarkably small eyes was a pair of large horns—the largest yet seen on a theropod. These horns may have been used in sexual display or in head-bashing combat for dominance over other members of the group. Almost as strange as the horns was the skull, which was tall and strong but with a weak lower jaw lined with rather slim teeth. Clearly, much remains to be learned about this peculiar meat-eater.

Physical Characteristics	40′ long. Deep but short skull; jaws lined with sharp, slender teeth. Large horns set above eyes.
Fossil Sites	Argentina.
Geologic Age	Early Cretaceous.

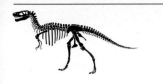

Ceratosaurus *Horned Reptile*
Saurischia; Theropoda; Carnosauria

Living at the same time and in some of the same areas as *Allosaurus, Ceratosaurus* was a much smaller and lighter meat-eater. For its size, though, it seems to have been an agile and fierce predator, with strong claws, a powerful jaw and remarkably large teeth. Excavations of trackways indicate that ceratosaurs may have hunted in packs and thus been able to bring down even the largest of prey. The use of a short, dull horn on the nose remains unclear; perhaps male ceratosaurs displayed their horns to attain dominance in a group.

Physical Characteristics	20′ long; powerfully built. Typically strong hind limbs; comparatively short and weak forelimbs; 4-fingered hands with sharp claws. Jaw massive but lightly built; teeth enormous, flattened. A row of bony spurs running down back and long tail may have supported a short fin or crest.
Fossil Sites	Colorado, USA; Tanzania, Africa.
Geologic Age	Late Jurassic.

Chasmosaurus *Ravine Reptile*
Ornithischia; Marginocephalia; Ceratopsia

All except the earliest ceratopsians, or horned dinosaurs, had a bony, skin-covered shield or frill sprouting from the back of the skull. *Chasmosaurus*'s long, impressive frill stretched over its neck and shoulders and was edged in bony knobs and short spikes. Had the frill been made of solid bone, it might have been too heavy for the dinosaur's strong neck muscles to support, but huge skin-covered holes made it easier to bear. Far too fragile to provide defense against the crushing jaws of a carnosaur, the frill may instead have been used mainly for display. Although neither the frill nor the blunt horn on *Chasmosaurus*'s nose would have provided sufficient protection against attack, the saberlike horns on its brows may have served as defensive weapons.

Physical Characteristics	17′ long. Typical ceratopsian shape: thick, strong legs; muscular neck; long, sloping skull culminating in a parrotlike beak.
Fossil Sites	Alberta, Canada.
Geologic Age	Late Cretaceous.

48

Chirostenotes *Slender Hands*
Saurischia; Theropoda; Coelurosauria

A little-known Late Cretaceous relative of *Oviraptor*—
which, with its short, deep head and extraordinary
toothless beak, was one of the oddest-looking of all
theropods—*Chirostenotes* was a comparatively small,
lightly built meat-eater, whose slender body was designed
for speed rather than power. It probably stalked and
chased down small prey such as lizards and small
mammals and perhaps stole eggs from other dinosaurs'
nests. *Chirostenotes* would have had to beware of the
extraordinary variety of great carnosaurs (such as
Albertosaurus) and sickle-clawed theropods (such as
Dromaeosaurus) that shared its Alberta terrain.

Physical Characteristics — Not well represented in fossil records. 7′ long (fossil finds
indicate that male and female *Chirostenotes* may have
differed markedly in size). Strong hind limbs; much
shorter forelimbs; slender, graceful clawed hands.

Fossil Sites — Alberta, Canada.

Geologic Age — Late Cretaceous.

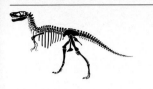

Coelophysis *Hollow Form*
Saurischia; Theropoda; Coelurosauria

An early coelurosaur, this slim, agile dinosaur must have been a formidable hunter. It had a streamlined, flexible body, sharp-clawed hands, and powerful jaws lined with dozens of sharp teeth, yet, because its bones were hollow, it weighed little more than 50 pounds. The famous 1947 discovery of more than 100 complete and partial *Coelophysis* skeletons in a single site at Ghost Ranch, New Mexico, included both adults and juveniles. This led scientists to surmise that this small predator may have traveled in groups and hunted in packs, making up in number and ferocity what it lacked in size and weight. Its forefeet were strong and supple enough to grasp prey.

Physical Characteristics	10′ long; 50 pounds. Tapering tail counterbalanced by long, slim neck; head slender, elongated; teeth serrated. Birdlike hind feet with 3 clawed toes; forefeet tipped with sharp claws.
Fossil Sites	New Mexico, Connecticut, USA; Zimbabwe, Africa.
Geologic Age	Late Triassic.

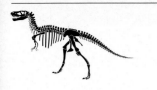

Compsognathus *Elegant Jaw*
Saurischia; Theropoda; Coelurosauria

One of the smallest dinosaurs yet discovered, this meat-eater probably grew to no more than 2′ long—about the size of a house cat. *Compsognathus* was a typical coelurosaur, built for speed and agility, which enabled it to chase down and snap up lizards and other small game. The fossilized bones of a lizard were found in the stomach of the most complete skeleton of a *Compsognathus* yet unearthed. Like many other small theropods, *Compsognathus* had skeletal features that more closely resembled modern birds than other modern reptiles. It shared the dry landscape of Late Jurassic Europe with *Archaeopteryx,* the famous feathered dinosaur.

Physical Characteristics	2′ long; 6½ pounds. Tail extremely long, tapering; strong, almost birdlike hind limbs with large, 3-toed feet; short forelimbs with 2 or 3 clawed fingers. Neck long and flexible; head fairly large; jaws armed with sharp teeth.
Fossil Sites	Germany and France.
Geologic Age	Late Jurassic.

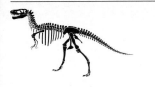

Daspletosaurus *Frightful Reptile*
Saurischia; Theropoda; Carnosauria

A close relative of *Tyrannosaurus, Daspletosaurus* was much smaller but seems to have been a remarkably powerful meat-eater, with a proportionately larger skull, a shorter, deeper jaw with larger teeth, and longer forelimbs than other carnosaurs. It lived side-by-side with, but was far less common than, the carnosaur *Albertosaurus,* which most likely feasted on abundant and vulnerable local duckbills. *Daspletosaurus*'s chief prey may have been the well-armed and comparatively uncommon ceratopsians (like the one pictured here) that shared its ecosystem.

Physical Characteristics	30′ long; 4 tons. Muscular tail; strong hind limbs; 3-toed hind feet; comparatively small forelimbs with 2 clawed fingers. Head huge; neck short and flexible. Teeth among the largest of those of any predatory dinosaur.
Fossil Sites	Alberta, Canada.
Geologic Age	Late Cretaceous.

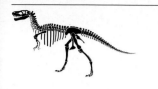

Deinonychus *Terrible Claw*
Saurischia; Theropoda; Coelurosauria

The discovery of the extraordinary *Deinonychus* in the 1960s helped redefine the popular image of dinosaurs as clumsy, lumbering behemoths that lived in a slow-motion world. The large-brained *Deinonychus,* with its lightweight skeleton made up of thinly walled bones like those of a bird, was designed for speed and agility; with its many formidable weapons, this dinosaur was clearly a fierce and fast-moving hunter. Some paleontologists surmise that *Deinonychus* may have hunted both alone and in packs, fearlessly attacking even much larger dinosaurs.

Physical Characteristics 13′ long; 150 pounds. Backward-curving, serrated teeth; strong forelimbs; grasping hands tipped with curved claws muscular hind limbs; spectacular, scythelike, 5″-long claw on each hind foot. Tail stiffened with bony rods to serve as a counterweight for balance; neck supple.

Fossil Sites Montana, Wyoming, USA.

Geologic Age Early Cretaceous.

Dilophosaurus *Two-ridged Reptile*
Saurischia; Theropoda; Ceratosauria

Although *Dilophosaurus* is classified as a ceratosaur, many of its features were similar to those found in the smaller coelurosaurs. Compared to other ceratosaurs, it was relatively lightly built, and its tail, neck, and forelimbs were long and slender. But *Dilophosaurus*'s distinguishing characteristic was a pair of thin, fragile ridges running along the top of its head and culminating in a short, backward-facing spike. This double crest, a seemingly non-utilitarian feature, may have been a secondary sexual characteristic occurring only in males. Male dilophosaurs may have shown off the crest to attract females or to establish dominance over other, less well-endowed males.

Physical Characteristics	20′ long. Its large head and strong jaws lined with knife-sharp teeth made it capable of attacking large dinosaurs. But its snout was unusually mobile, as if designed for the quick and agile movements required to grab smaller prey.
Fossil Sites	Arizona, USA.
Geologic Age	Early Jurassic.

Diplodocus *Double Beam*
Saurischia; Sauropodomorpha; Sauropoda

Although it reached 100′ in length, *Diplodocus* weighed only about a third of what the 70′-long *Apatosaurus* weighed. Almost all of *Diplodocus*'s length was taken up by its extremely long neck, which might have grown 20′ long, and its tapered whiplike tail, which grew 40′ long or more. With its long neck, and perhaps by rearing up on its hind legs, *Diplodocus* could have reached treetops beyond the grasp of most other plant-eating dinosaurs, gaining access to its choice of leaves and other vegetation. Given its size, *Diplodocus* must have feared few predators except *Allosaurus,* and may have been able to keep even this carnosaur at bay with vicious swipes of its extraordinary tail.

Physical Characteristics	100′ long; 12 tons. Neck and tail very long; extremely small body rarely exceeding 13′ long. Head tiny; little more than 2′ long. Peglike teeth used to scrape vegetation from branches.
Fossil Sites	Wyoming, Oklahoma, Utah, Colorado, USA.
Geologic Age	Late Jurassic.

Dromaeosaurus *Running Reptile*
Saurischia; Theropoda; Coelurosauria

Although smaller than its fierce relative *Deinonychus,*
Dromaeosaurus had many of the same characteristics:
speed, agility, specialized curved claws on the second toe of
each foot, a large brain, and, possibly, warm bloodedness.
But *Dromaeosaurus,* shown here eating a young hadrosaur,
also shared some attributes with the giant carnosaurs,
including a large skull and unusually large teeth. Whether
Dromaeosaurus hunted different prey than its larger
cousin remains unknown.

Physical Characteristics	Not well represented in fossil finds; only the skull and a few other bones have been found. Probably about 6′ long. Specialized claw, so spectacular in *Deinonychus,* probably far less impressive in this genus. Teeth larger than its relatives.
Fossil Sites	Alberta, Canada.
Geologic Age	Late Cretaceous.

Edmontosaurus *Edmonton Reptile*
Ornithischia; Ornithopoda; Hadrosauridae

One of the largest and latest of the duckbills, and closely related to *Anatosaurus, Edmontosaurus* was one of several similar genera that shared the same Late Cretaceous landscape in what is now Alberta, Canada. As many as 1,000 teeth packed *Edmontosaurus*'s cheeks, and its jaw was specially designed to allow the upper teeth to grind against the lower as the dinosaur chewed. Even the coarsest of plant material—pine needles, nuts, horsetails—could not have withstood this grinding motion. *Edmontosaurus* was one of the few hadrosaurids that bore no facial crest.

Physical Characteristics	43′ long; 3½ tons. Typical hadrosaurid: long, thick tail; strong hind limbs; smaller forelimbs sometimes used for quadrupedal motion; flattened head sloped down to a typically toothless beak.
Fossil Sites	Alberta, Canada.
Geologic Age	Late Cretaceous.

Euoplocephalus *Well-armored Head*
Ornithischia; Thyreophora; Ankylosauridae

Well armored and as solid as tanks, *Euoplocephalus* and other ankylosaurs were plant-eaters that bore an extraordinary array of defenses. *Euoplocephalus* was smaller than the huge carnosaurs and with its massive hips and short legs was one of the slowest of dinosaurs. But even the most determined predator, like the *Albertosaurus* pictured here, would have trouble conquering this dinosaur. *Euoplocephalus*'s equipment included bands of bony armor interspersed with bony protrusions along the back, head, and neck. The tail bore a huge club that most likely served as a formidable defensive weapon.

Physical Characteristics	18′ long; 3 tons. Bony plates, equipped with knobs and spikes, covered its back; larger plates protected the neck; bony spines protruded at the shoulders and the base of the tail. Head, virtually enclosed in armor, featured long cheek spikes and bony protective plates. Tail club, formed of fused bone, large and heavy.
Fossil Sites	Alberta, Canada.
Geologic Age	Late Cretaceous.

68

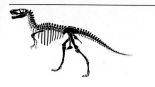

Gallimimus *Rooster Mimic*
Saurischia; Theropoda; Ornithomimidae

Gallimimus and the other ornithomimosaurs—also known as ostrich dinosaurs—were among the fastest and most agile of all dinosaurs. A streamlined creature that may have been able to attain racehorse speeds, *Gallimimus* was among the largest of its kind, though its forefeet were weaker than those of other ornithomimosaurs. While scientists cannot be certain what *Gallimimus* ate, it probably snapped up insects, lizards, and other small prey with quick motions of its toothless beak. Scanning its forested surroundings for prey and potential threats, sprinting away on slender, muscular legs at the first sign of danger, it would have closely resembled a modern ostrich.

Physical Characteristics	13' long. Slim legs; long, whiplike neck; large, keen eyes; large brain. Long, thin forelimbs ended in 3 attenuated, clawed fingers.
Fossil Sites	Mongolia.
Geologic Age	Late Cretaceous.

Gryposaurus *Curved Reptile*
Ornithischia; Ornithopoda; Hadrosauridae

No dinosaurs were more common and well adapted to Late Cretaceous Asia and North America than the hadrosaurids or duck-billed dinosaurs. The area that now stretches from Alberta, Canada, to the badlands of Montana was host to *Maiasaura, Anatosaurus, Edmontosaurus,* and *Gryposaurus,* a large, typical duckbill. *Gryposaurus*'s distinguishing feature was a large mass of solid bone set on the snout in front of its eyes. Paleontologists guess that this strange hump was not likely to have been an effective deterrent to attacking carnosaurs and other predators; instead, it may have served for sexual display.

Physical Characteristics	Up to 30′ long. A typical duckbill: strong, hoofed hind limbs; forefeet tipped with hooflike nails. Would have been comfortable walking on either 2 or 4 legs.
Fossil Sites	Alberta, Canada; Montana, New Mexico, USA.
Geologic Age	Late Cretaceous.

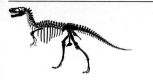

Herrerasaurus *Herrera Reptile*
Primitive Dinosaur

Among the oldest dinosaurs yet discovered, *Herrerasaurus* is thought to have been one of the few known ancestors of both Ornithischian and Saurischian dinosaurs. It would have shared its range with primitive reptile relatives of both dinosaurs and mammals which did not survive the end of the Triassic period. A lightweight dinosaur, *Herrerasaurus* wouldn't have been able to tackle very large prey, but its sickle-shaped teeth were clearly designed for eating meat.

Physical Characteristics	10′ long; 220 pounds; stockily built. Long hind limbs, substantially shorter forelimbs, and structure of backbone surprisingly similar to those of much more advanced theropods.
Fossil Sites	Argentina.
Geologic Age	Late Triassic.

Heterodontosaurus *Mixed-tooth Reptile*
Ornithischia; Ornithopoda; Heterodontosauridae

Most dinosaurs had only one type of tooth, but the unusual early ornithopod *Heterodontosaurus* had three types, as, coincidentally, many mammals do. The first type, set in the front of its upper jaw, were small, pointed cutting teeth, similar to a mammal's incisors; the toothless bottom jaw was formed into a hard beak. The second type, perhaps present only in males, were sharp, short tusks in the upper and lower jaws, similar to mammalian canine teeth; the lower pair fitted into slots in the upper jaw, and the upper pair probably protruded from the dinosaur's closed mouth. Finally, both sexes had broad, molarlike cheek teeth. Scientists think that the front teeth were used to nip off leaves, the canines to chop the leaves into pieces, and the cheek teeth to grind up the vegetation.

Physical Characteristics	4′ long; lightly built. Strong hind limbs; smaller forelimbs with clawed fingers; sloping skull.
Fossil Sites	South Africa.
Geologic Age	Late Jurassic.

76

Homalocephale *Even Head*
Ornithischia; Marginocephalia; Pachycephalosauridae

Few ornithopods were stranger-looking than the pachycephalosaurs (bone-headed dinosaurs), distinguished by their immensely thick skulls. Many bonehead skulls had huge domes, but *Homalocephale*'s skull, although characteristically thickened, was wedge-shaped and dotted with bony knobs. Many paleontologists think that boneheads' heavy skulls may have served a social purpose, since they clearly did not evolve as an aid to feeding or as a defense against predators. *Homalocephale* may have lived in herds or family groups headed by a single dominant male. To determine dominance in the herd, *Homalocephale* males may have banged heads. More remarkable than the cranial features were *Homalocephale*'s extremely wide hips, which have led some experts to speculate that these dinosaurs gave birth to live young.

Physical Characteristics	10' long. Largely bipedal; strong hind limbs; much smaller forelimbs; tail stiff and muscular.
Fossil Sites	Mongolia.
Geologic Age	Late Cretaceous.

78

Huayangosaurus *Huayang Reptile*
Ornithischia; Thyreophora; Stegosauridae

Of the numerous fascinating and mysterious dinosaur
fossils unearthed in Asia, many have been found in
mainland China in recent years. One fascinating find was
Huayangosaurus, first described in 1982. This stegosaur
had the typical body plan of its suborder, but had one
unusual feature: While other stegosaurs had toothless
beaks, *Huayangosaurus* had weak teeth in the front of
its mouth. Paleontologists believe that *Huayangosaurus*
may have been an early, primitive stegosaur, and that the
toothless beak of later stegosaurs was an evolutionary
adaptation. Like its descendents, *Huayangosaurus*
probably spent the vast majority of its time on
4 legs, perhaps rising onto its hind limbs to browse
on succulent vegetation.

Physical Characteristics	13′ long; a small stegosaur. Thick body; tiny head; plates and spines running along its back and tail.
Fossil Sites	Shanxi, China.
Geologic Age	Middle Jurassic.

Hypacrosaurus *Very High-ridged Reptile*
Ornithischia; Ornithopoda; Hadrosauridae

While many duckbills had facial or cranial crests, none had showier crests than *Hypacrosaurus* and its relatives, the lambeosaurine duckbills. *Hypacrosaurus*'s crest, larger in males than females, was short and squat in comparison to that of some lambeosaurines and culminated in a bony spike that aimed down the dinosaur's back. *Hypacrosaurus* also had specialized extensions of the vertebrae along the back that undoubtedly supported a ridge of skin, which may have served as a heat regulator. By turning the ridge toward the sun, *Hypacrosaurus* would have absorbed warmth through the extra skin; by turning away, it would have allowed excess heat to escape.

Physical Characteristics	30' long; a typically large Late Cretaceous duckbill. Built for bipedal locomotion, it could also move on all fours. Jaws contained masses of ridged teeth for grinding coarse vegetation. Crest hollow.
Fossil Sites	Alberta, Canada; Montana, USA.
Geologic Age	Late Cretaceous.

82

Hypsilophodon *High-ridged Tooth*
Ornithischia; Ornithopoda; Hypsilophodontidae

The word "ornithopod" conjures up images of heavy-bodied
duckbills lacking speed and grace. But not all ornithopods
fit that image; some early ornithopods, ancestors of the
duckbills, were among the fleetest of all dinosaurs. One
such ornithopod was *Hypsilophodon*, swift as a gazelle,
with long legs and a stiff tail used as a counterweight for
balance. As it was a plant-eater, it must have used its speed
as a means of evading predators. *Hypsilophodon* may
have had bony scales running down its back, providing at
least modest protection against an attacker's jaws. A find
of 20 *Hypsilophodon* fossils in one site revealed that this
small dinosaur probably lived in herds or family groups,
much as modern gazelles do.

Physical Characteristics	5–7½′ long. Long, slender hind limbs with 4-toed feet; shorter forelimbs with 5-fingered hands. Horny beak; incisor-like teeth in upper jaw, ridged teeth located in cheeks, adapted for grinding vegetation.
Fossil Sites	South Dakota, USA; England; Portugal.
Geologic Age	Early Cretaceous.

Iguanodon *Iguana Tooth*
Ornithischia; Ornithopoda; Iguanodontidae

Unearthed in 1809, fossils of this well-known ornithopod, a plant-eating denizen of wet lowlands, were among the earliest dinosaur remains discovered. Initially scientists believed that the giant bones and teeth may have come from a huge mammal, but in 1825 fossil-hunter Gideon Mantell theorized that the teeth belonged to a reptile resembling the modern-day iguana. Thus came the name and the first, very inaccurate reconstruction of *Iguanodon* as an enormous, bulky lizard with elephantine legs, virtually no neck, and a horn on its nose. The "horn" was actually a thumb spike, found on both forefeet, that may have been used in defense against predators or in sexual skirmishes.

Physical Characteristics	30′ long; 5 tons. A typical large ornithopod: large, strong hind limbs; relatively long forelimbs; 5-fingered hands; stiff tail.
Fossil Sites	Utah, USA; England; Belgium; Germany; Mongolia; Tunisia.
Geologic Age	Early Cretaceous.

Lambeosaurus *Lambe's Reptile*
Ornithischia; Ornithopoda; Hadrosauridae

Many Late Cretaceous duckbills had extraordinary crests, but *Lambeosaurus* had one of the oddest of all, a hollow, hatchet-shaped protrusion of bone situated atop its skull, between the eyes. A solid spike behind the crest pointed backward and may have supported a ridge of skin running along the animal's back. The nasal passages ran through the crest, perhaps allowing *Lambeosaurus* to produce loud resonant honks and bellows. The hollow crest may also have served as a heat exchanger, ventilating excess heat in midday and collecting warmth during cooler hours.

Physical Characteristics	Different species of *Lambeosaurus* may have differed greatly in size; some grew about 30′ long, but at least one (found in Baja California) seems to have reached more than 50′ long, making it the largest of all duckbills. *Lambeosaurus* was similar to other duckbills but had a particularly long and flexible neck.
Fossil Sites	Alberta, Saskatchewan, Canada; Montana, USA; Baja California, Mexico.
Geologic Age	Late Cretaceous.

Lesothosaurus *Lesotho Reptile*
Primitive Ornithischia; No defined group

Lesothosaurus (thought to be the same dinosaur as one known as *Fabrosaurus*) was small and lightweight, barely bigger than a small dog. It may have resembled a large modern lizard, but it had strong hind limbs (the shins of which were longer than the thighs) and a strong, tapering tail; it probably spent most of its time on hind legs. All these features indicate that *Lesothosaurus* was a speedy denizen of ancient plains, utilizing its quickness to escape from predators. Scientists think that all later ornithischians, from the massive ankylosaurs to the fleet hypsilophodonts, may have evolved from the fabrosaurids.

Physical Characteristics   3′ long. 4-toed hind feet tipped with claws, would have provided traction for running. Smaller forelimbs with 5 clawed fingers might have been used to gather food. Unusual teeth, smooth and sharp in front, shaped like arrowheads along the side, probably served to chop and tear vegetation.

Fossil Sites   Lesotho, Africa.

Geologic Age   Early Jurassic.

Maiasaura *Good-mother Reptile*
Ornithischia; Ornithopoda; Hadrosauridae

The discovery of *Maiasaura* marks one of the most excitin
recent chapters in the history of paleontology. Since 1979
scientists have unearthed an enormous trove of fossils,
including the skeletons of thousands of young and adult
maiasaurs, fossilized mud nests, and eggshell fragments.
These finds revealed that *Maiasaura* nested in colonies an
were the first evidence that any dinosaurs had done so. The
presence of partly grown juveniles still in the nest indicate
that parent maiasaurs cared for their young, bringing food
to the nest for months or even years, as birds and mammal
do. Previously, scientists had assumed that all dinosaurs
merely laid their eggs and then abandoned them, as do
most modern reptiles.

Physical Characteristics	30' long. A typical duckbill: long, slender hind limbs; smalle forelimbs; stiff, flattened tail used as a counterweight. Usually bipedal, could also move on 4 legs. Front jaw toothless; rear jaw bore hundreds of flattened teeth.
Fossil Sites	Montana, USA.
Geologic Age	Late Cretaceous.

Mamenchisaurus *Mamenchin Reptile*
Saurischia; Sauropodomorpha; Sauropoda

The illustration opposite readily demonstrates what set
Mamenchisaurus apart from all other dinosaurs: its neck.
While all sauropods were distinguished by long necks,
Mamenchisaurus had the proportionately longest neck of
any known animal in the history of life on earth. At half the
dinosaur's total length, the neck may have conveyed one
important advantage: *Mamenchisaurus* could easily grasp
treetop needles and other vegetation that even other long-
necked sauropods would have had difficulty reaching.

Physical | 72' long. Neck 36' long, with 19 vertebrae (more than
Characteristics | any other dinosaur), each more than twice as long as the
vertebrae in the back. Bony protrusions allowed the neck
vertebrae to overlap, forming a strong, though stiff,
support; openings in the vertebrae helped lighten the
neck's weight.

Fossil Sites | Mamenchi, China.

Geologic Age | Late Jurassic.

Nanotyrannus *Pygmy Tyrant*
Saurischia; Theropoda; Carnosauria

In 1988 a team of paleontologists announced the
"discovery" of a new dinosaur genus: *Nanotyrannus*, a
much smaller cousin of the famous *Tyrannosaurus rex.*
Yet the actual unearthing of *Nanotyrannus* had taken
place nearly half a century earlier. Its skull (the only
fossil yet found) had languished for 46 years in a museum,
misidentified as that of a small albertosaur. Some scientists
still believe that the skull belongs to a young albertosaur,
but others believe that tooth-wear patterns indicate the
individual was an adult, and that many of the skull's
features were remarkably similar to those found in the
great tyrannosaurs, rather than the albertosaurs. The skull
also suggests that *Nanotyrannus* was related to the
smaller predator *Troödon.*

Physical Characteristics	17′ long. Large braincase; long, narrow snout; sharp, curved teeth. Eyes forward facing, which some scientists believe would have given it stereoscopic vision, as modern mammals have.
Fossil Sites	Montana, USA.
Geologic Age	Late Cretaceous.

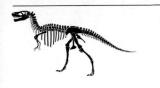

Ornitholestes *Bird Robber*
Saurischia; Theropoda; Coelurosauria

The fossil beds of the Morrison Formation in the western United States contained the remains of many giant dinosaurs: *Allosaurus, Diplodocus,* and *Stegosaurus* are just three of the famous behemoths that roamed this landscape in the Late Jurassic period. Among the few small dinosaurs found in the formation was *Ornitholestes,* a predator built more for speed than for strength or ferocity. It may have behaved similarly to the way a jackal does, catching large insects, lizards, and small mammals, feasting on carrion, and perhaps snatching an unwary bird or baby dinosaur when it had the chance. Its speed and agility would have allowed it to evade the area's large meat-eaters.

Physical Characteristics	6½′ long. Strong, slender tail; streamlined hind limbs; grasping forefeet. Teeth rather small.
Fossil Sites	Wyoming, USA.
Geologic Age	Late Jurassic.

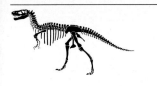

Ornithomimus *Bird Mimic*
Saurischia; Theropoda; Ornithomimidae

Resembling ostriches and similar terrestrial birds, *Ornithomimus* had strong, slender legs designed for quick and agile movement; an extraordinarily long and skinny neck; and a small head equipped with a toothless beak and keen, watchful eyes. These features suggest that *Ornithomimus* may have been able to swing its head down to browse on vegetation or snap up insects and other small creatures, then quickly raise its head above the level of nearby bushes to scan for danger. Upon spying an *Albertosaurus* or another predator *Ornithomimus* would have sprinted away—and few hunters would have been able to keep up.

Physical Characteristics | 13′ long. Large, flexible hips; long, slender tail used as a counterweight; strong hind limbs; 3 toes on each hind foot. Long-fingered hands, built for grasping, might have helped it gather vegetation or unearth buried eggs.

Fossil Sites | Alberta, Canada; Colorado, Utah, USA; Mongolia.

Geologic Age | Late Cretaceous.

Orodromeus *Mountain Runner*
Ornithischia; Ornithopoda; Hypsilophodontidae

Perhaps the most famous dinosaur discovery of the past
two decades was the unearthing of *Maiasaura,* a find that
provided crucial evidence that some dinosaurs nested
colonially and cared for their young. Another recently
discovered dinosaur shared *Maiasaura's* upland haunts in
what is now Montana: *Orodromeus,* a slim, agile, and fast-
moving hypsilophodontid. *Orodromeus* also nested in
groups, laying eggs in careful spiral clutches and possibly
tending them after laying. Fossil evidence suggests that
Orodromeus young didn't remain in the nest long after
hatching, as *Maiasaura* young did.

Physical Characteristics	7′ long. Strong hind limbs with long shins; tail stiff for balance. Ridged cheek teeth, probably used to chew vegetation, insects, and small crustaceans.
Fossil Sites	Montana, USA.
Geologic Age	Late Cretaceous.

Ouranosaurus *Brave Reptile*
Ornithischia; Ornithopoda; Iguanodontidae

Though in many ways a typical iguanodontid, *Ouranosaurus* had one distinguishing feature: tall spines protruded from its vertebrae and ran from its shoulders to halfway down the tail, most likely supporting a sail of skin similar to that found in the carnosaur *Spinosaurus*. The sail probably served to regulate the dinosaur's internal heat in the hot African terrain. Turned toward the sun in early morning, the sail would have provided a large skin surface for the absorption of heat; turned away from the sun at midday, it would vent unwanted (and potentially dangerous) heat.

Physical Characteristics	23′ long. Flexible neck; sloping skull with a flattened snout and (possibly) a crest, similar to crests found frequently in the duckbills, later ornithopods. The 5-fingered forefeet had small walking hooves on 2 toes.
Fossil Sites	Niger.
Geologic Age	Early Cretaceous.

Oviraptor *Egg Robber*
Saurischia; Theropoda; Coelurosauria

A beaked, nearly toothless theropod, *Oviraptor* was similar in some ways to the fierce *Deinonychus* and other sickle-clawed dinosaurs. It had no claw, however, and its tail lacked the bony sheaths that gave the sickle-claws their balance and agility. Its short, deep beak was quite powerful, however, and may have been designed for crushing tough vegetation or even bones. The crest on its head could not have served any purpose in foraging or defense; perhaps it was a secondary sexual characteristic, used for display.

Physical Characteristics	6′ long. Head short, with flattened crest near the nasal region. Strong hind limbs; 3 large, clawed toes, tiny first toe. Particularly strong shoulders, arms, and 3-fingered hands, designed for grasping. Curved jaws more powerful than those of many of its kin.
Fossil Sites	Mongolia.
Geologic Age	Late Cretaceous.

Pachycephalosaurus *Thick-headed Reptile*
Ornithischia; Marginocephalia; Pachycephalosauridae

Few dinosaurs presented odder profiles than the
pachycephalosaurids, or bone-headed dinosaurs. The skull
of plant-eating *Pachycephalosaurus*, the largest of the
boneheads, rose in an extraordinary, solid-bone dome on
top. This high bony dome, obviously having no influence on
the dinosaur's ability to find food and providing little
defense against predators, was almost certainly a
secondary sexual characteristic. Some scientists believe
that male pachycephalosaurs may have engaged in
tremendous head-butting battles for dominance in the
herd, fierce clashes echoed today among bighorn sheep and
other herding animals.

Physical Characteristics	15′ long. Skull topped with 10″-thick dome ornamented with small knobs and spines. Resembled other ornithopods: strong hind limbs; smaller forelimbs equipped with clasping hands. Clearly a bipedal forager of plants, seeds, and other vegetation.
Fossil Sites	Alberta, Canada.
Geologic Age	Late Cretaceous.

108

Pachyrhinosaurus *Thick-nosed Reptile*
Ornithischia; Marginocephalia; Ceratopsia

Not all ceratopsians, or horned dinosaurs, actually had horns. Instead of the sharp spikes seen in *Triceratops* and others, the mid-size ceratopsian *Pachyrhinosaurus* had a thick, bulging mass of bone above and between the eyes. This bony pad would not have provided much defense against *Tyrannosaurus* and other predators that ranged across the same landscape as *Pachyrhinosaurus.* Some scientists postulate that the pad might have served the same purpose as the bony domes of the bone-headed dinosaurs: to serve as protection during head-butting clashes between males vying for domination in a herd.

Physical Characteristics	18′ long. Thick legs; hoofed toes. Skull huge (4′ long); bony mass on snout. Neck frill, so dramatic in some ceratopsians, modest.
Fossil Sites	Alberta, Canada.
Geologic Age	Late Cretaceous.

Panoplosaurus *Armored Reptile*
Ornithischia; Thyreophora; Ankylosauridae

Some dinosaurs used speed as a means of evading
predators, while others may have relied on eyesight or
an acute sense of smell. Ankylosaurs, heavy-bodied,
slow-moving, and heavily armored everywhere but on
the inaccessible belly, survived by presenting virtually
impregnable defenses. *Panoplosaurus,* a late nodosaurid
ankylosaur, may also have wielded the sharp spikes lining
its shoulders and sides as active weapons. Shifting in place
to meet an attacking carnosaur, this comparatively small
ankylosaur may have kept its spikes in the way of the
predator's sharp-toothed jaws, perhaps even jabbing when
given the opportunity. Like others of its kind, it probably
ate low-lying plants and other vegetation.

Physical Characteristics	Up to 23' long; 4 tons. Back covered with solid bony plates and studs; thick plates of armor fused to skull. Heavy skull armor lightened by cavities in the bone structure.
Fossil Sites	Alberta, Canada; Montana, South Dakota, Texas, USA.
Geologic Age	Late Cretaceous.

112

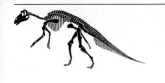

Parasaurolophus *Beside Saurolophus*
Ornithischia; Ornithopoda; Hadrosauridae

No duckbill had a more spectacular crest than
Parasaurolophus. Remarkably, its crest, jutting
backward from the skull, contained paired nasal passages
that ran from the nostrils to the top of the crest, then
back down again to the head. This odd design may have
served *Parasaurolophus* as an echo chamber, allowing
it to produce loud, deep bellows in sexual display or
communication with the herd. Some scientists think
that a frill of skin may have connected *Parasaurolophus*'s
crest to its neck. The many blood vessels and mucous
membranes within the crest may have allowed it to serve
as a heat exchanger, as did the great skin sails of
Ouranosaurus and *Spinosaurus*.

Physical Characteristics	33′ long; a typically large and heavy-bodied duckbill. Crest 6′ long, hollow, spike-shaped.
Fossil Sites	Alberta, Canada; New Mexico, Utah, USA.
Geologic Age	Late Cretaceous.

Pinacosaurus *Board Reptile*
Ornithischia; Thyreophora; Ankylosauridae

Many armored dinosaurs fall into the group known
as ankylosaurs. Although all ankylosaurs had a roughly
similar body plan, at least two different families existed.
The family Nodosauridae included *Panoplosaurus*
and others that had long spikes along their flanks.
Pinacosaurus belonged to the second family,
Ankylosauridae, which included many genera with
smaller spikes but heavy clubs at the tips of their tails.
As slow-moving as its relatives, *Pinacosaurus* may
have used its club as a defensive weapon, swinging it
back and forth to keep predators at bay.

Physical Characteristics | 18' long; a mid-size ankylosaur, rather lightly built. Large skull armored with bony plates; rounded beak; tiny teeth suitable for cropping vegetation. Tail ended in large club made of fused bone. *Pinacosaurus* had an odd third nostril, the purpose of which remains a mystery.

Fossil Sites | Mongolia; northern China.

Geologic Age | Late Cretaceous.

Plateosaurus *Flat Reptile*
Saurischia; Sauropodomorpha; Prosauropoda

The prosauropod infraorder contains types of dinosaurs ranging from agile, flesh-eating predators to heavy-bodied plant-eaters. *Plateosaurus,* the best known of all the prosauropods, belonged to the latter group. It is likely that *Plateosaurus* behaved much like a sauropod, moving about the Mesozoic landscape in herds, rising freely on its hindlimbs or using its long neck to reach treetop vegetation. Yet most scientists no longer believe that the prosauropods were the direct ancestors of the sauropods; it is now thought that the two groups may have evolved from a common smaller ancestor.

Physical Characteristics
More than 26' long; a large prosauropod. Legs less pillarlike than those of sauropods. Strong jaws and abundant leaf-shaped teeth designed for eating such tough plants as cycads and conifers. Short hands with widespread fingers tipped with long claws; "thumb" claw very large and curved.

Fossil Sites
England; France; Germany; Switzerland.

Geologic Age
Late Triassic.

118

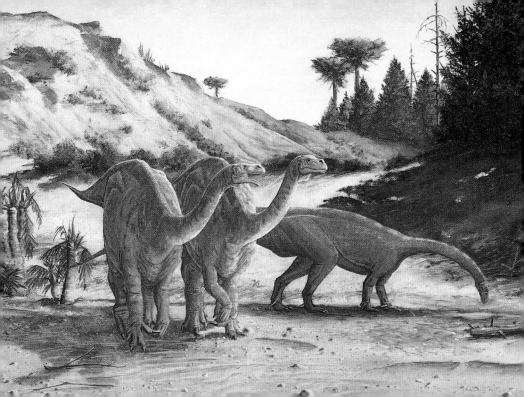

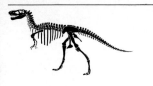

Protoavis *First Bird*
Saurischia; Theropoda; Coelurosauria

For decades *Archaeopteryx* had been considered the dinosaur most closely related to modern birds. But *Protoavis,* discovered in 1986, may have had an even more exciting mix of dinosaur and bird features, yet it appeared more than 200 million years ago—75 million years before *Archaeopteryx.* Scientists remain sharply divided over *Protoavis*'s characteristics, with many claiming that it was simply a small theropod without clear affinity to birds. Only further study—and perhaps further fossil finds— will help determine what role (if any) *Protoavis* assumed in the evolution of dinosaurs into birds.

Physical Characteristics	18″ long; tiny for a dinosaur, roughly the size of a modern-day crow. Strong hind limbs, bony tail, saurischian pelvis all clearly reptilian. Large eye sockets, hollow bones, strong wishbone, and breastbone featuring a keel. Tiny, sharp teeth crammed in the front of its jaw indicate that it ate insects and other small prey.
Fossil Sites	Texas, USA.
Geologic Age	Late Triassic.

120

Protoceratops *First Horned Face*
Ornithischia; Marginocephalia; Ceratopsia

The ceratopsians, or horned dinosaurs, were the last ornithischian dinosaurs to evolve, first appearing in the Late Cretaceous period and disappearing at the period's end. *Protoceratops,* an early, primitive ceratopsian, didn't actually have horns at all, but merely bore a raised crestlike ridge on its nose and bumps above its eyes. *Protoceratops* did have the characteristic ceratopsian neck frill, which anchored the jaw muscles and may also have functioned as a heat exchanger. Interestingly, *Protoceratops*'s hind limbs were much longer than its forelimbs; some scientists believe that it could have risen onto 2 legs at times, unlike the clearly 4-legged ceratopsians that evolved later. A nest containing hatched and unhatched *Protoceratops* eggs, discovered in the 1920s, were the first dinosaur eggs ever found.

Physical Characteristics	9′ long; a small ceratopsian. Typical hard beak; numerous cheek teeth; powerful jaw muscles.
Fossil Sites	Mongolia.
Geologic Age	Late Cretaceous.

Psittacosaurus *Parrot Reptile*
Ornithischia; Marginocephalia; Ceratopsia

Psittacosaurus and its relatives, known as a group as the "parrot dinosaurs," are the most primitive ceratopsians yet found, and may have been the ancestors of later horned dinosaurs. *Psittacosaurus* had a bony, square head and a hard beak, as did the typical ceratopsians, but there were important skeletal differences between the two groups, too. *Psittacosaurus*'s hind limbs were much longer than its forelimbs, for example, and its overall body shape was more similar to that of an ornithopod than a later ceratopsian. *Psittacosaurus* may have been comfortable walking on either two or four legs as it searched for the leaves and other vegetation that were its food.

Physical Characteristics	6′ long; a small ceratopsian. Skull similar to those of the horned dinosaurs: spikelike cheekbones; possibly a small nasal horn; a ridge of bone on the back of the skull served to anchor the muscles of the lower jaws, as did the ceratopsians' neck frills.
Fossil Sites	China; Mongolia; Siberia.
Geologic Age	Early Cretaceous.

124

Rhabdodon *Rod Tooth*
Ornithischia; Ornithopoda; Iguanodontidae

Rhabdodon, fossils of which have been found in the
Transylvania region of Romania, was an unusual dinosaur
in many ways, and its classification has been controversial.
Without doubt, it was a bipedal plant-eater, as were the
Iguanodon and other ornithopods that predated the
familiar duck-billed dinosaurs. Over the past decade,
however, experts studying the skull and skeleton of
Rhabdodon have pointed out that its large, compact jaw,
the placement of its teeth, and other features indicate
that it also resembled the hypsilophodonts. Final judgment
of *Rhabdodon*'s exact place in the dinosaur family tree,
however, awaits further research or the discovery of
new fossils.

Physical Characteristics	13′ long; a small iguanodontid. Solidly built; spent most of its time on 2 legs. Toothless beak; grinding cheek teeth.
Fossil Sites	Romania.
Geologic Age	Late Cretaceous.

126

Saltasaurus *Salta Reptile*
Saurischia; Sauropodomorpha; Sauropoda

It's tempting to identify groups of dinosaurs by a single characteristic: Ceratopsians had horns; carnosaurs had long, knifelike teeth; sauropods had long necks and tails. But classifying dinosaurs isn't that simple, and occasionally confounding evidence turns up. *Saltasaurus,* for example, was an armored sauropod, bearing thousands of tiny bony plates set closely together in the skin of its back. These plates, some of which may have borne short spikes, probably served to protect this slow-moving sauropod from the jaws of large carnosaurs. *Saltasaurus* was a comparatively small sauropod, as were many members of its family, Titanosauridae, the last group of sauropods to evolve.

Physical Characteristics	40′ long. Neck slim, shorter than the necks of many other sauropods; tail long and flexible; hind limbs longer than forelimbs. Armored plates, some no more than ¼″ in diameter, others reaching about 4″, covered its back.
Fossil Sites	Argentina.
Geologic Age	Late Cretaceous.

128

Saurolophus *Crested Reptile*
Ornithischia; Ornithopoda; Hadrosauridae

Though lacking the spectacular adornments of some other duck-billed dinosaurs, *Saurolophus* also had a large skull culminating in a bony spike (an extension of the nasal bones) that pointed backward from the top of the head. *Saurolophus*'s nasal passages apparently ran through the spike, perhaps functioning to amplify sounds produced by this duckbill. The loud honks produced may have kept herds in communication in dense forest. Some scientists believe that there may have been large pouches of skin on the spike that when inflated would amplify the dinosaur's calls even further.

Physical Characteristics	30–39′ long, depending on species. Strong, flattened tail; slender limbs; hoofed toes and fingers. Long, sloping skull had a spike in the back; toothless beak; abundant grinding cheek teeth.
Fossil Sites	Alberta, Canada; Montana, USA; Mongolia.
Geologic Age	Late Cretaceous.

Sauropelta *Shielded Reptile*
Ornithischia; Thyreophora; Ankylosauridae

Sauropelta belonged to the nodosaurid family of
ankylosaurs, as did *Panoplosaurus,* but lived much earlier
than its relative. *Sauropelta* was typically well armored, its
back and tail covered with bony plates, and its sides
guarded by sharp spikes. Although not invulnerable—
ankylosaurs probably fell prey to marauding theropods on
occasion—slow-moving *Sauropelta* would have defended
itself passively, depending on its armor to convince
predators to seek easier prey.

Physical Characteristics	20′ long; 3 tons or more; one of the largest nodosaurids. Armor set in bands across back and tail. Legs slimmer than those of later ankylosaurs; skull long and slender. No bony club on the tip of its tail.
Fossil Sites	Montana, USA.
Geologic Age	Early Cretaceous.

Scelidosaurus *Limb Reptile*
Ornithischia; Primitive Thyreophoran

One of the earliest ornithischian dinosaurs, *Scelidosaurus* seems to have been a primitive relative of both the better-known armored dinosaurs (ankylosaurs) and plated dinosaurs (stegosaurs). Currently, most scientists consider it most closely related to the ankylosaurs. *Scelidosaurus* didn't have the extensive bony plates seen in *Panoplosaurus* and other, later ankylosaur genera, but had bony studs set in the skin and probably rows of short spikes. Its head ended in a typically toothless beak, with which it could tear off vegetation that would then be chewed by weak, leaf-shaped teeth set back in the jaws.

Physical Characteristics	11' long. Heavy, massive body; strong legs; small head. Hi bones lacked the prepubic process (a bone that jutted forward) found in other ornithischians.
Fossil Sites	England; Tibet.
Geologic Age	Early Jurassic.

Scutellosaurus *Little Shielded Reptile*
Ornithischia; Primitive Thyreophoran

Scutellosaurus, a primitive relative of armored and plated dinosaurs, had hundreds of bony studs set in the skin of its back. *Scutellosaurus* could not have depended on its studs to protect it from the powerful jaws and razor-sharp teeth of the theropods that hunted it, but perhaps its modest armor would have been enough to deflect the first bite, allowing *Scutellosaurus* to escape or convincing a hungry theropod to pursue easier prey. Aside from its armor, its most distinctive feature was its disproportionately long tail.

Physical Characteristics	4′ long; slim-bodied and agile. Surprisingly long forelimbs indicate it may have spent more time on all fours than most of its relatives did.
Fossil Sites	Arizona, USA.
Geologic Age	Early Jurassic.

Segnosaurus *Slow Reptile*
Saurischia; Sauropodomorpha; Prosauropoda

For many years after its discovery in the 1970s, scientists believed that *Segnosaurus* was a classificatory anomaly: a plant-eating theropod. But more recent analysis reveals that this large dinosaur and its kin were most likely actually Late Cretaceous prosauropods—but no less bizarre for the new identification. A saurischian dinosaur with the hipbone and toothless beak of an ornithischian, and sharp teeth in the back of its jaw, *Segnosaurus* remains a puzzling, hard-to-categorize member of the ever-changing dinosaur family tree. Evidence suggests that *Segnosaurus* may have dwelt near swamps and lakes; some scientists think that its toes were webbed.

Physical Characteristics	30′ long; the largest segnosaurid yet discovered. *Segnosaurus* had strong, clawed, 4-toed feet— a prosauropod trait.
Fossil Sites	Mongolia.
Geologic Age	Late Cretaceous.

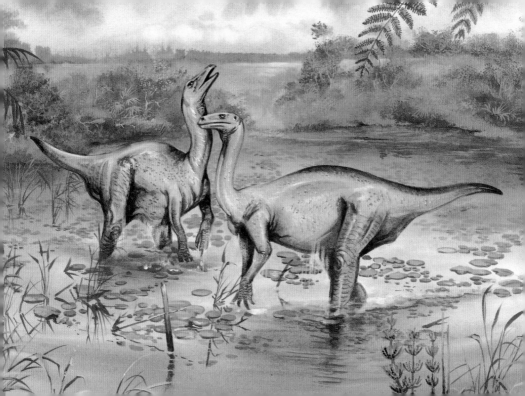

Seismosaurus *Earthquake Reptile*
Saurischia; Sauropodomorpha; Sauropoda

With the 1985 discovery of this remarkable dinosaur, paleontologists began to re-estimate the outside limits of sauropod size. Previously it was believed that *Diplodocus* was the longest of dinosaurs. But *Seismosaurus* may have grown a third longer—making it by far the longest land animal in the history of the earth. Its great size could have enabled it to reach succulent vegetation far beyond the reach of even other sauropods. Watching one of these earth-shaking reptiles striding across the Late Jurassic landscape would have provided a spectacular sight.

Physical Characteristics	Up to 130′ long; 100 tons. Typical diplodocid sauropod: extremely long neck (35-40′ long) and tail; slender body; tiny head. Each of the great vertebrae supporting its heavy tail was more than 1′ long.
Fossil Sites	New Mexico, USA.
Geologic Age	Late Jurassic.

Shunosaurus *Sichuan Reptile*
Saurischia; Sauropodomorpha; Sauropoda

Abundant fossil finds show that *Shunosaurus* must have been one of the most common dinosaurs living in what is now Sichuan during mid-Jurassic times, and may have lived in herds, as did other sauropods. It is possible that *Shunosaurus* had a club at the end of its tail, which it may have used as a defensive weapon when attacked by carnosaurs. If so, it is one of the only sauropods known to have evolved this adaptation. Some scientists believe that this primitive sauropodomorph may have inhabited a dinosaur infraorder between prosauropods and sauropods.

Physical Characteristics	33′ long; a small sauropod. Large head; comparatively short neck and tail. Thick legs like those of other sauropods.
Fossil Sites	Sichuan, China.
Geologic Age	Middle Jurassic.

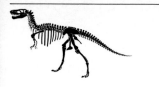

Spinosaurus *Spiny Reptile*
Saurischia; Theropoda; Carnosauria

Spinosaurus was an unusual-looking carnosaur with a tall sail of skin running along its back from the shoulders to the base of the tail. The sail may have helped this giant carnosaur regulate its body temperature, as did the skin sails of other dinosaurs. Turned toward the sun in the cool of morning, the vein-rich sail would have absorbed heat quickly; turned away at midday, it would have quickly vented potentially dangerous excess heat.

Physical Characteristics	40' long; one of the largest carnosaurs, but apparently more lightly built and less powerful than the allosaurs that shared its African home. Skin sail supported by strong spines up to 6' high extending from the backbone. Teeth, unusual for those of a carnosaur, were straight rather than curved.
Fossil Sites	Niger; Egypt.
Geologic Age	Middle to Late Cretaceous.

Staurikosaurus *Cross Reptile*
Primitive Dinosaur

An early, very primitive dinosaur, *Staurikosaurus* exhibited skeletal and other features that would have been seen later in the two saurischian suborders, plant-eating sauropodomorphs and meat-eating theropods. *Staurikosaurus* was very lightly built and seems to have been a quick, agile predator. Interestingly, its large head and sharp, curved teeth indicate that it may have preyed on relatively large animals, including other small dinosaurs. Despite its speed, it was probably hunted by some of the larger predators of its time, particularly the heavy-bodied "thecodonts," reptile rulers of the Mesozoic before the rise of the dinosaurs.

Physical Characteristics	6′ long; 70 pounds. Small bipedal dinosaur: muscular, slim hind limbs; short forelimbs with 5-fingered hands; slender, tapering tail.
Fossil Sites	Brazil.
Geologic Age	Late Triassic.

Stegoceras *Covered Horn*
Ornithischia; Marginocephalia; Pachycephalosauridae

One of the few well-known pachycephalosaurids, or bonehead dinosaurs, *Stegoceras* had a far less dramatically thickened skull than did its famous relative *Pachycephalosaurus.* Nevertheless, its skull had a similar raised dome of solid bone, which may have evolved to protect the dinosaur during intraspecies head-butting, such as during battles for dominance by rival males. The thick skull would have protected the brain, while also (along with the spine) diffusing the impact of the crash. *Stegoceras* may have wandered the plains of North America in small herds or family groups, seeking vegetation and trying to avoid the attention of local carnosaurs and sickle-clawed theropods.

Physical Characteristics	6½′ long; a heavy-bodied ornithopod. Strong tail; powerful hind limbs with 3 large toes on each foot; smaller forelimbs, possibly 5-fingered hands. Bumps and short spikes on back of skull.
Fossil Sites	Alberta, Canada.
Geologic Age	Late Cretaceous.

Stegosaurus *Plated Reptile*
Ornithischia; Thyreophora; Stegosauridae

This powerfully built herbivore was the largest and is the best known of all the plated dinosaurs. The stegosaurs were among the slowest of all dinosaurs, yet *Stegosaurus* and its kin apparently did not have the defenses that other slow-moving dinosaurs had, such as the bony, virtually impregnable armor of the ankylosaurs. Most paleontologists believe that *Stegosaurus*'s plates were too flimsy to provide a useful defense, and that they probably functioned as heat exchangers, as did the great skin sail of *Spinosaurus*. *Stegosaurus* probably used its heavy tail, lined with sharp spikes, to protect itself from hungry predators.

Physical Characteristics	30′ long. Huge, heavy body; small head; sloping skull; small, blunt teeth. Hind limbs more than twice as long as the forelimbs; may have stood on 2 legs on occasion.
Fossil Sites	Colorado, Oklahoma, Utah, Wyoming, USA.
Geologic Age	Late Jurassic.

Stygimoloch *River Styx Devil*
Ornithischia; Marginocephalia; Pachycephalosauridae

Every pachycephalosaurid featured a remarkable skull topped with a thick mass of bone. *Stygimoloch*, described and named in 1983, may have been the most spectacular of the lot: Its bare, egg-shaped dome was surrounded by bony studs and clusters of horns, some of which may have been 6″ long or longer. *Stygimoloch*'s dome would have protected the skull during intraspecies head-butting competitions undertaken by males battling for supremacy in the herd. The horns may have served as weapons of intimidation and could have inflicted severe damage in battles.

Physical Characteristics	5′ long; a small pachycephalosaurid. Sturdily built; bipedal. Jaws lined with small but sharp teeth.
Fossil Sites	Montana, USA.
Geologic Age	Late Cretaceous.

Styracosaurus *Spiked Reptile*
Ornithischia; Marginocephalia; Ceratopsia

Styracosaurus was among the most spectacular-looking of all the horned dinosaurs, bearing a long, sharp snout horn, a smaller horn above each eye, and an extraordinarily ornate and convoluted neck frill. Across the top of its elaborate frill were 6 main spikes pointing up and back, while along its edges were smaller spikes and bumps. The bones of the frill had 2 large openings that lightened the structure but also rendered it useless as armor; instead, the dinosaur's powerful jaw muscles may have attached to the frill. *Styracosaurus* must have defended itself with its sharp nose horn, which was capable of ripping the flesh of an attacking theropod. The frill's spikes most likely would have intimidated all but the most ambitious predators.

Physical Characteristics	18′ long; a medium-size heavy-bodied ceratopsian. Huge head, horny beak; strong legs with hoofed feet; thick tail.
Fossil Sites	Alberta, Canada; Montana, USA.
Geologic Age	Late Cretaceous.

Telmatosaurus *Marsh Reptile*
Ornithischia; Ornithopoda; Hadrosauridae

The dominant dinosaurs of Late Cretaceous North America were the hadrosaurids, or duck-billed dinosaurs. Fossils of such hadrosaurids as *Lambeosaurus* and *Parasaurolophus*, among others, have been found at the Judith River Formation of Alberta, Canada. *Telmatosaurus* was an unusual duckbill in that it lived in Late Cretaceous Europe. The climate and vegetation of that continent must not have been as welcoming to the duckbills as were those of North America. In other ways, however, *Telmatosaurus* followed the typical hadrosaurid body plan.

Physical Characteristics	30′ long; an average-size hadrosaurid. Heavy-bodied; strong, slender hind limbs; long, flattened tail. Skull deep and narrow.
Fossil Sites	France; Hungary.
Geologic Age	Late Cretaceous.

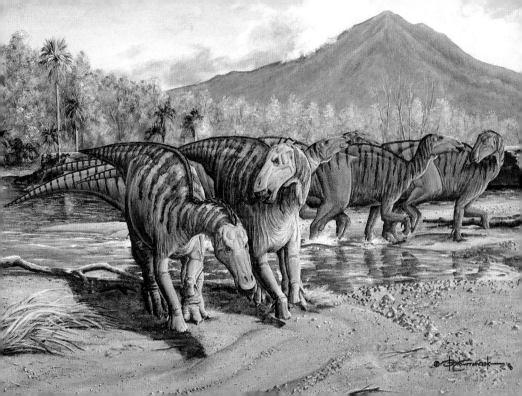

Tenontosaurus *Sinew Reptile*
Ornithischia; Ornithopoda; Hypsilophodontidae

Tenontosaurus was a strange yet fascinating dinosaur whose skeletal features have led some paleontologists to place it with the iguanodontids. Most experts, however, now believe *Tenontosaurus* was an atypical, gigantic hypsilophodontid, much larger than any other yet discovered. An exciting fossil find in Montana unearthed a skeleton of *Tenontosaurus* surrounded by 5 skeletons of *Deinonychus,* the fierce sickle-clawed hunter. Although the fossils may have ended up in the same bone bed by coincidence, it is possible that packs of *Deinonychus* attacked the far larger *Tenontosaurus,* much as packs of wolves will overcome a moose or caribou today.

Physical Characteristics	24′ long. Strong legs; flexible neck; remarkably long, heavy tail took up more than half the dinosaur's length. Unlike other hypsilophodontids, *Tenontosaurus* probably spent most of its time on all fours.
Fossil Sites	Montana, Oklahoma, Texas, Arizona, USA.
Geologic Age	Early Cretaceous.

158

Thescelosaurus *Wonderful Reptile*
Ornithischia; Ornithopoda; Hypsilophodontidae

Like *Tenontosaurus*, *Thescelosaurus*, a bipedal plant-eater, appears to have been most closely allied to the hypsilophodontids. But it also had several unusual characteristics, such as teeth in the front of its upper jaw, 5-toed feet, and long thigh bones, which indicate that it was not as fleet-footed as the hypsilophodontids. *Thescelosaurus* had rows of bony studs set into the skin of its back that may have offered protection from some predators it was unable to outrun.

Physical Characteristics	11' long; a mid-size dinosaur. Strode on its strong hind limbs; used its shorter forelimbs and 5-fingered hands to gather plants for food. Stiff tail served as a counterbalance
Fossil Sites	Alberta, Saskatchewan, Canada; Montana, Wyoming, USA
Geologic Age	Late Cretaceous.

Triceratops *Three-horned Face*
Ornithischia; Marginocephalia; Ceratopsia

Triceratops, the largest and heaviest—and now the
most famous—horned dinosaur, was also one of the most
abundant; so many fossils have been found in certain areas
that many scientists believe that *Triceratops* traveled
in great herds. *Tyrannosaurus* and *Albertosaurus*
probably preyed on the vast assemblages of *Triceratops.*
This horned dinosaur must have been quite capable of
defending itself with its enormous brow horns, some of
which may have reached 4′ (or more) in length.

Physical Characteristics	The largest of the 15 or so *Triceratops* species grew to 30′ long and weighed 6 tons. Huge head; long, sharp horns above eyes; shorter horn on nose; short, solid-bone frill.
Fossil Sites	Alberta, Saskatchewan, Canada; South Dakota, Montana, Wyoming, Colorado, USA.
Geologic Age	Late Cretaceous.

Troödon *Wounding Tooth*
Saurischia; Theropoda; Coelurosauria

This strange dinosaur with knifelike teeth was long
believed to be a hypsilophodontid and the only flesh-eating
ornithischian. Now, though, many paleontologists place
Troödon among such agile, large-brained, sickle-clawed
predators as *Dromaeosaurus*. Interestingly, *Troödon*
appears to have had many skeletal similarities to modern
birds, though without feathers. *Troödon* lived at the same
time and in the same locations as *Maiasaura* and may
have utilized its speed, teeth, and sickle claws to raid
Maiasaura nests for juveniles.

Physical Characteristics	8' long. Lightly built, but formidably armed with long, sharp, serrated teeth and sickle claws. *Troödon* may have had binocular vision, a great advantage for a predator.
Fossil Sites	Alberta, Canada; Montana, USA.
Geologic Age	Late Cretaceous.

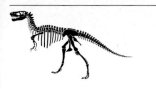

Tyrannosaurus *Tyrant Reptile*
Saurischia; Theropoda; Carnosauria

Undoubtedly the most famous of all dinosaurs, *Tyrannosaurus* was also one of the largest and most powerful of the carnosaurs. *Tyrannosaurus* was so large, in fact, that some scientists believe that it couldn't have moved quickly enough to have been an effective predator and must have been a carrion-eater. Following close skeletal study, however, some paleontologists believe that *Tyrannosaurus* (shown competing with other predators) was actually a tremendously strong hunter, equipped with extraordinarily powerful jaws and serrated teeth up to 7″ long. Packs of tyrannosaurs may have preyed on the abundant *Triceratops* by chasing a stampeding herd, choosing a single victim, and then confronting its deadly horns in a battle unparalleled among dinosaurs.

Physical Characteristics	40′ long or more; 4–8 tons. Hind limbs powerfully muscular; forelimbs short but comparatively strong. Skull 4′ long; great jaws anchored by tremendous muscles.
Fossil Sites	Alberta, Canada; Montana, possibly New Mexico, USA.
Geologic Age	Late Cretaceous.

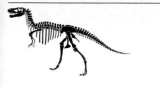

Velociraptor *Swift Robber*
Saurischia; Theropoda; Coelurosauria

This predator was comparatively small for a dinosaur but very powerful for its size. Like the larger *Deinonychus*, *Velociraptor* was well equipped for hunting. Its large brain enabled it to utilize its weaponry to bring down prey far larger than itself. One remarkable fossil find in Mongolia revealed a *Velociraptor* locked in combat with the horned dinosaur *Protoceratops;* each presumably had succeeded in killing the other during a battle.

Physical Characteristics	7′ long. Strong, clawed, grasping hands; muscular hind limbs, each tipped with a large sickle claw. Long, low skull; possibly binocular vision. Jaws lined with knife-sharp teeth. Birdlike features included, most notably, a large breastbone.
Fossil Sites	Mongolia.
Geologic Age	Late Cretaceous.

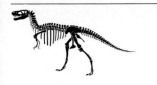

Yangchuanosaurus *Yang-ch'üan Reptile*
Saurischia; Theropoda; Carnosauria

Although not as massive as the later tyrannosaurs,
Yangchuanosaurus and the other allosaurids were the
greatest and most widespread carnosaurs of the Late
Jurassic period. *Yangchuanosaurus* was designed for
hunting big game and clearly was capable of attacking and
conquering large stegosaurs. Some experts believe that
allosaurids may have hunted in packs, an added adaptation
that would have made *Yangchuanosaurus* a virtually
unstoppable predator.

Physical Characteristics	33' long; smaller than *Allosaurus*. Strong hind limbs; flexible neck; powerful jaws lined with particularly large, sharp, serrated teeth. Very long, muscular, laterally flattened tail for balance. Huge skull topped with 2 parallel ridges and a pair of short horns.
Fossil Sites	Sichuan, China.
Geologic Age	Late Jurassic.

Yunnanosaurus *Yunnan Reptile*
Saurischia; Sauropodomorpha; Prosauropoda

A close relative of the famous *Plateosaurus,* but smaller and less well known, *Yunnanosaurus* was among the first prosauropods to be discovered in China. Like its relatives, *Yunnanosaurus* presented a vaguely sauropod-like profile, and was probably also a comparatively slow-moving plant-eater. Oddly, however, *Yunnanosaurus*'s evenly spaced teeth were sharp enough to eat meat. *Yunnanosaurus,* as with all the prosauropods (except the controversial segnosaurs), did not survive the Early Jurassic period.

Physical Characteristics
20′ long, a large plateosaurid. Resembled the later sauropods, but had a much shorter neck. Hind limbs strong and typically large; broad forefeet indicate that it probably spent most of its time on all fours but was able to rise onto its hind limbs to reach desirable vegetation.

Fossil Sites
Yunnan, China.

Geologic Age
Late Triassic/Early Jurassic.

Family Tree

Order	Ornithischia			
Suborder	Marginocephalia		Ornithopoda	
Family	Ceratopsia	Pachycephalosauridae	Camptosauridae	Hadrosauridae
Genus	Chasmosaurus Pachyrhinosaurus Protoceratops Psittacosaurus Styracosaurus Triceratops	Homalocephale Pachycephalosaurus Stegoceras Stygimoloch	Camptosaurus	Anatosaurus Edmontosaurus Gryposaurus Hypacrosaurus Lambeosaurus Maiasaura Parasaurolophus Saurolophus Telmatosaurus

			Thyreophora	
Heterodontosauridae	Hypsilophodontidae	Iguanodontidae	Ankylosauridae	Stegosauridae
Heterodontosaurus	Hypsilophodon Orodromeus Tenontosaurus Thescelosaurus	Iguanodon Ouranosaurus Rhabdodon	Euoplocephalus Panoplosaurus Pinacosaurus Sauropelta	Huayangosaurus Stegosaurus

Order	Saurischia			
Suborder	Theropoda			
Infraorder	Carnosauria	Ceratosauria	Coelurosauria	Ornithomimidae
Genus	Acrocanthosaurus Albertosaurus Allosaurus Carnotaurus Ceratosaurus Daspletosaurus Nanotyrannus Spinosaurus Tyrannosaurus Yangchuanosaurus	Dilophosaurus	Archaeopteryx Avimimus Chirostenotes Coelophysis Compsognathus Deinonychus Dromaeosaurus Ornitholestes Oviraptor Protoavis Troödon Velociraptor	Gallimimus Ornithomimus

Sauropodomorpha	
Prosauropoda	Sauropoda
Anchisaurus	Apatosaurus
Plateosaurus	Barosaurus
Segnosaurus	Brachiosaurus
Yunnanosaurus	Camarasaurus
	Diplodocus
	Mamenchisaurus
	Saltasaurus
	Seismosaurus
	Shunosaurus

Time Line	Late Triassic	Late Triassic to Early Jurassic
	Coelophysis Herrerasaurus Plateosaurus Protoavis Staurikosaurus	Anchisaurus Yunnanosaurus

Early Jurassic	Middle Jurassic	Late Jurassic
Dilophosaurus	Huayangosaurus	Apatosaurus
Lesothosaurus	Shunosaurus	Archaeopteryx
Scelidosaurus		Barosaurus
Scutellosaurus		Brachiosaurus
Yangchuanosaurus		Camarasaurus
		Compsognathus
		Diplodocus
		Heterodontosaurus
		Mamenchisaurus
		Ornitholestes
		Seismosaurus
		Stegosaurus

Late Jurassic to Early Cretaceous	Early Cretaceous	Middle to Late Cretaceous
Allosaurus	Acrocanthosaurus Baryonyx Carnotosaurus Deinonychus Hypsilophodon Iguanodon Ouranosaurus Psittacosaurus Sauropelta Tenontosaurus	Spinosaurus

Late Cretaceous

Albertosaurus
Anatosaurus
Avimimus
Camptosaurus
Ceratosaurus
Chasmosaurus
Chirostenotes
Daspletosaurus
Dromaeosaurus
Edmontosaurus
Euoplocephalus
Gallimimus
Gryposaurus
Homalocephale
Hypacrosaurus
Lambeosaurus
Maiasaura
Nanotyrannus
Ornithomimus
Orodromeus

Oviraptor
Pachycephalosaurus
Pachyrhinosaurus
Panoplosaurus
Parasaurolophus
Pinacosaurus
Protoceratops
Rhabdodon
Saltasaurus
Saurolophus
Segnosaurus
Stegoceras
Stygimoloch
Styracosaurus
Telmatosaurus
Thescelosaurus
Triceratops
Troödon
Tyrannosaurus
Velociraptor

Dinosaur Skeletons

Many important characteristics of the different dinosaur suborders are revealed in their skeletons. These drawings represent some frequently seen dinosaur body types. A skeleton appears with each text account to show you the dinosaur's general body structure. Wide variations may occur from genus to genus.

Stegosaurus

The strong, thick legs and heavy body of this *Stegosaurus* reveal that it was a comparatively slow-moving dinosaur that walked on four legs. Its small jaw, designed for eating vegetation, shows that *Stegosaurus* must have spent muc of each day feeding.

All thyreophorans in the text are keyed to this image.

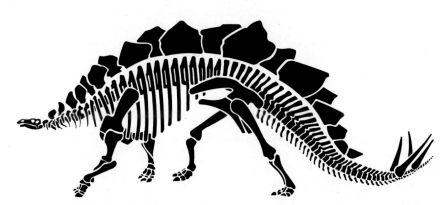

Triceratops

As the skeleton shows, this large horned dinosaur walked on four legs, and may have been capable of substantial speed. Like many other ceratopsians, it had a massive neck frill, perhaps used for defense, as a heat regulator, or simply for display. Two horns on its brow were anchored to a skeletal spike.

All marginocephalians in the text are keyed to this image.

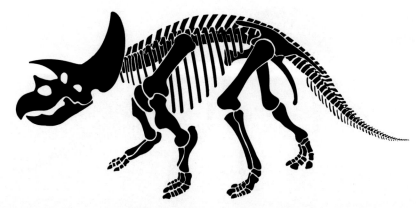

Maiasaura

Like other hadrosaurs, *Maiasaura* had a heavy body, a strong tail, powerful hind legs, and shorter forelimbs. It may have spent much of its time walking on two legs, perhaps dropping to four on occasion. Its large, beaked jaw was designed for eating tough vegetation.

All ornithopods in the text are keyed to this image.

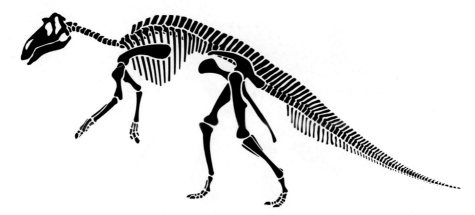

Euoplocephalus

Another low-slung plant-eater, *Euoplocephalus* and other ankylosaurs featured sturdy legs and a strong neck. While the bony plates in its armor were not skeletal features, the club at the end of its tail was clearly a solid mass of bone. Ankylosaurs may have used these clubs to ward off attacks by hungry carnosaurs and other predators.

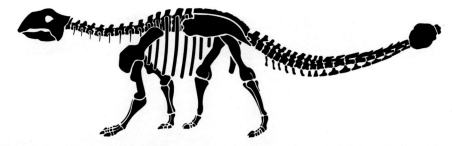

185

Albertosaurus

Albertosaurus's extraordinarily powerful hind legs, flexible neck, and, of course, massive jaws lined with knifelike teeth all mark it as a meat-eater, and (almost certainly) as a deadly hunter. While chasing down prey, this carnosaur may have used its tapering tail as a counterweight.

All theropods in the text are keyed to this image.

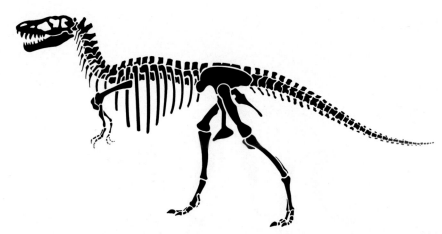

Ornithomimus

Most small theropods were spectacularly fleet and agile hunters. As this skeleton shows, many had slender but muscular legs, long-fingered grasping hands, and a tapering tail (sometimes strengthened with bony rods) used for balance. Some, like *Ornithomimus,* had toothless, beaked jaws, while others (such as *Deinonychus*) had jaws lined with sharp, serrated teeth.

Camarasaurus
All sauropods had thick, pillarlike legs, long, tapering tails, and long, slender necks culminating in deep, short jaws. These features may have allowed the sauropods to reach tender treetop vegetation far beyond the grasp of other plant-eating dinosaurs. All sauropodomorphs (prosauropods and sauropods) in the text are keyed to this image.

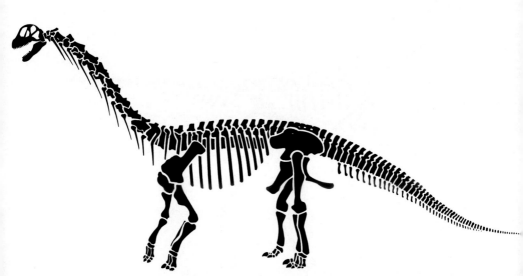

A
Acrocanthosaurus, 18
Albertosaurus, 20
Allosaurus, 22
Anatosaurus, 24
Anchisaurus, 26
Apatosaurus, 28
Archaeopteryx, 30
Avimimus, 32

B
Barosaurus, 34
Baryonyx, 36
Brachiosaurus, 38
Brontosaurus, 28

C
Camarasaurus, 40
Camptosaurus, 42
Carnotaurus, 44
Ceratosaurus, 46
Chasmosaurus, 48
Chirostenotes, 50
Coelophysis, 52
Compsognathus, 54

D
Daspletosaurus, 56
Deinonychus, 58
Dilophosaurus, 60
Diplodocus, 62
Dromaeosaurus, 64

E
Edmontosaurus, 66
Euoplocephalus, 68

G
Gallimimus, 70
Gryposaurus, 72

H
Herrerasaurus, 74
Heterodontosaurus, 76
Homalocephale, 78
Huayangosaurus, 80
Hypacrosaurus, 82
Hypsilophodon, 84

I
Iguanodon, 86

L
Lambeosaurus, 88
Lesothosaurus, 90

M
Maiasaura, 92
Mamenchisaurus, 94

N
Nanotyrannus, 96

O
Ornitholestes, 98
Ornithomimus, 100
Orodromeus, 102
Ouranosaurus, 104
Oviraptor, 106

P
Pachycephalosaurus, 108
Pachyrhinosaurus, 110
Panoplosaurus, 112
Parasaurolophus, 114
Pinacosaurus, 116
Plateosaurus, 118
Protoavis, 120
Protoceratops, 122
Psittacosaurus, 124

R
Rhabdodon, 126

S
Saltasaurus, 128
Saurolophus, 130
Sauropelta, 132
Scelidosaurus, 134
Scutellosaurus, 136
Segnosaurus, 138
Seismosaurus, 140
Shunosaurus, 142
Spinosaurus, 144
Staurikosaurus, 146
Stegoceras, 148
Stegosaurus, 150
Stygimoloch, 152
Styracosaurus, 154

T
Telmatosaurus, 156
Tenontosaurus, 158
Thescelosaurus, 160
Triceratops, 162
Troödon, 164
Tyrannosaurus, 166

V
Velociraptor, 168

Y
Yangchuanosaurus, 170
Yunnanosaurus, 172

Credits

Illustrators hold copyrights to their works.

Donna Braginetz (65, 73, 103, 105, 135)
Michael Cole (35, 143)
Brian Franczak (21, 25–29, 33, 37–41, 45, 47, 51–57, 61, 63, 67, 69, 89–93, 97, 101, 107, 109, 113, 115, 119, 123–129, 137, 141, 149–157, 161–169, 173)
Edward Heck (81)
Douglas Henderson (59)
Frank Ippolito (31, 71, 99, 121)
Eleanor M. Kish, reproduced with permission of Canadian Museum of Nature, Ottawa, Canada (133, 159)
Vladimir Krb (43, 77, 111, 117, 171)
Michael Rothman (85, 87, 95)
Jan Sovak (19, 23, 49, 75, 79, 83, 131, 139, 145, 147)

Skeleton drawings by
Kris Ellingsen

Consultant
Philip J. Currie, Royal Tyrrell Museum, Alberta, Canada

Chanticleer Staff
Publisher: Andrew Stewart
Managing Editor: Barbara Sturman
Editor: Jane Mintzer Hoffman
Designer: Sheila Ross
Photo Editor: Timothy Allan
Production: Gretchen Bailey Wohlgemuth
Editorial Assistant: Kate Jacobs

Founding Publisher: Paul Steiner
Series Design: Massimo Vignelli

The National Audubon Society

The NATIONAL AUDUBON SOCIETY is in the vanguard of the environmental movement. Its more than 600,000 members, 14 regional and state offices, extensive chapter networks in the United States and Latin America, and a professional staff of scientists, lobbyists, lawyers, policy analysts, and educators are fighting to save threatened ecosystems and to restore the natural balance that is critical to the quality of life on our planet. The society's system of sanctuaries protects more than a quarter-million acres of essential habitat and unique natural areas for birds, wild animals, and rare plant life.

The National Audubon Society publishes the award-winning *Audubon* magazine; *Audubon Activist,* a monthly newsjournal; *American Birds,* an ornithological journal; and *Audubon Adventures,* a children's nature newsletter. In addition, its award-winning Audubon television specials deal with a variety of environmental themes.

For more information, contact the National Audubon Society at 700 Broadway, New York, New York 10003. (212) 832-3200.